Fish, Fish, Fish!

by Rachel Russ

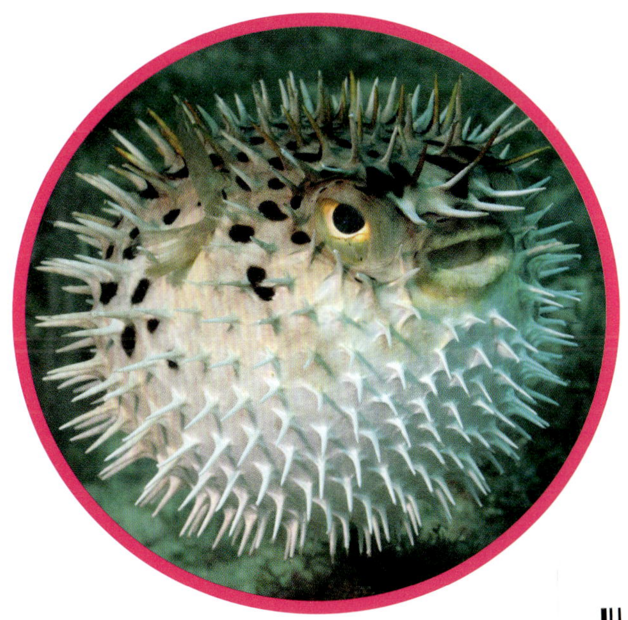

OXFORD
UNIVERSITY PRESS

Lots Of Fish!

See the fish.

Fish can be quick.

Fish can be long.

Fish can be odd!

Quick Fish

The sailfish is quick!
See its sail and its bill.

The sailfish seeks lots of fish.

The sailfish rushes in. It hits the fish with its bill.

Long Fish

The eel is a long, thin fish.

It waits in the rocks.
Then it pops up at night.

Odd Fish

This odd fish is a batfish.
It has red lips!

This fish puffs up.
It is toxic.

This fish has big fins.
The fins can be legs!

This odd fish is a boxfish.

This fish hops along the mud.

Fab Fish

Fish can be lots of things.

Fish can be fab!

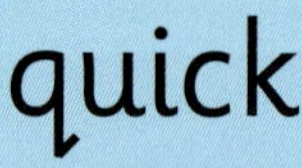

quick

long

odd

toxic

Encourage students to match the words to the pictures.